ALFRED'S BASIC BASS METHOD 1

THE MOST POPULAR METHOD FOR LEARNING HOW TO PLAY

For individual or class instruction

RON MANUS

& L.C. HARNSBERGER

Alfred Music
P.O. Box 10003
Van Nuys, CA 91410-0003
alfred.com

ISBN-10: 0-7390-4885-6 (Book)   ISBN-10: 0-7390-4886-4 (Book & CD)   ISBN-10: 0-7390-4887-2 (Book & DVD)
ISBN-13: 978-0-7390-4885-6 (Book)   ISBN-13: 978-0-7390-4886-3 (Book & CD)   ISBN-13: 978-0-7390-4887-0 (Book & DVD)

ISBN-10: 0-7390-4942-9 (DVD)   ISBN-10: 0-7390-4943-7 (CD)
ISBN-13: 978-0-7390-4942-6 (DVD)   ISBN-13: 978-0-7390-4943-3 (CD)

Cover Photos courtesy of Daisy Rock Guitars

2

Contents

Parts of the Bass

Parts of the Amp

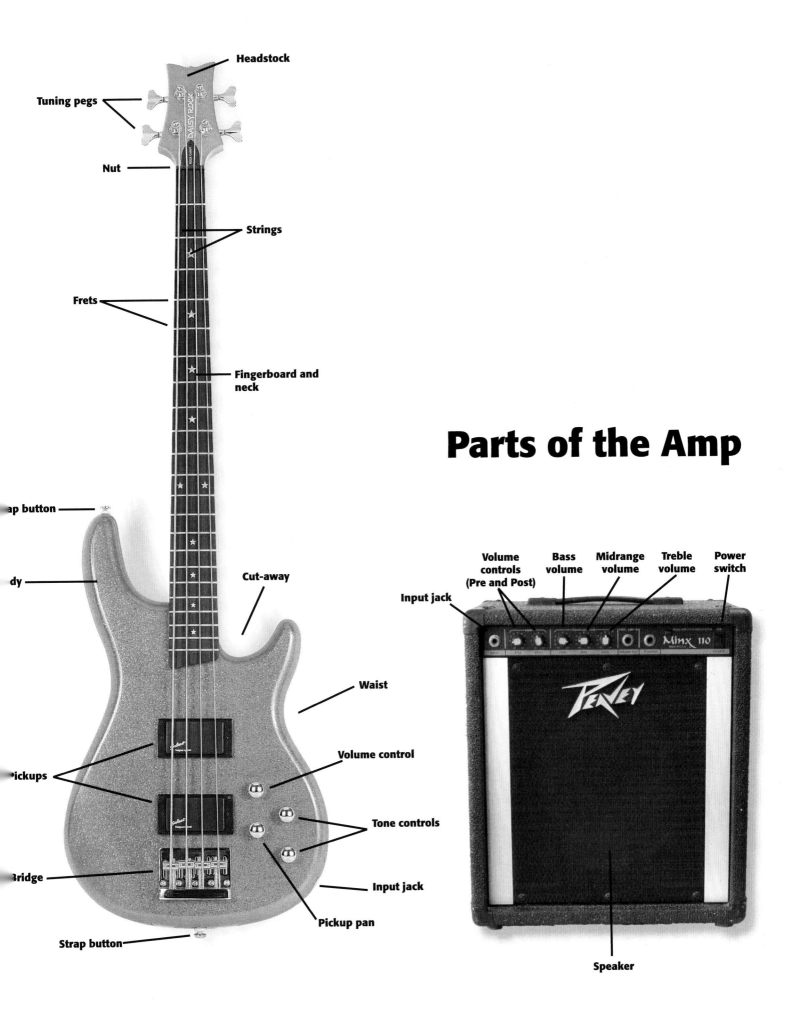

Headstock

Tuning pegs

Nut

Strings

Frets

Fingerboard and neck

ap button

dy

Cut-away

Waist

Volume control

ickups

Tone controls

Bridge

Input jack

Pickup pan

Strap button

Volume controls (Pre and Post)

Input jack

Bass volume

Midrange volume

Treble volume

Power switch

Speaker

How to Hold Your Bass

Below are two ways to hold your bass.
Pick the one that is most comfortable for you.

Sitting.

Standing with strap.

The Right Hand

Proper Hand Position

There are two common ways of playing the strings. One is with your fingers, and the other is with a pick. Using your fingers may give you more speed and flexibility where playing with a pick will give you a very sharp attack and brighter sound.

Using Your Fingers

Most players alternate their index and middle fingers to pluck the strings. If you aren't comfortable using two fingers, start off using only one finger, and add the other later. When playing with your fingers, it is important to notice that after striking the string, the finger comes to a rest on the next string except when playing the fourth string, where the finger rests on the pickup.

Index finger

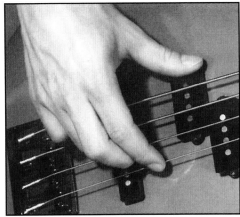

In position.

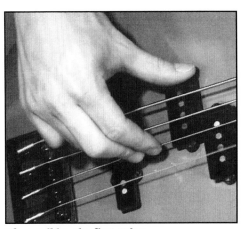

After striking the first string.

Middle finger

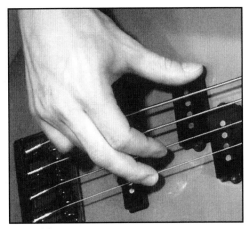

In position.

After striking the first string.

To get used to playing with the fingers, play a series of notes on an open string slowly and evenly. Do this with all four open strings.

Using a Pick

Hold the pick between your thumb and index finger. Hold it firmly, but don't squeeze it too hard.

To get used to playing with a pick, play a series of notes on an open string slowly and evenly. Do this with all four open strings.

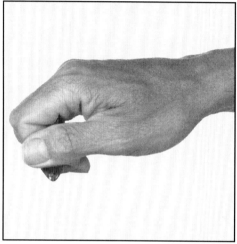
Holding the pick.

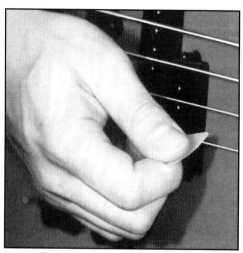
In position.

After striking the first string.

The Left Hand

Proper Hand Position

Learning to use your left-hand fingers starts with a good hand position. Place your hand so your thumb rests comfortably in the middle of the back of the neck. Position your fingers on the front of the neck as if you are gently squeezing a ball between them and your thumb. Keep your elbow in and your fingers curved.

Keep your elbow in and fingers curved.

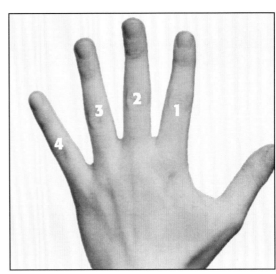

Numbers of the left-hand fingers.

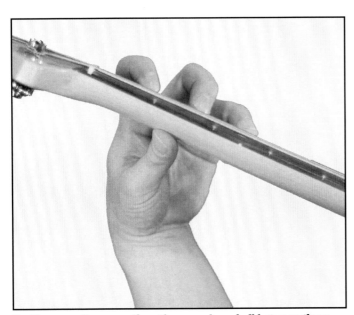

Position your fingers as if gently squeezing a ball between them and your thumb.

Placing a Finger on a String

When you press a string with a left-hand finger, make sure you press firmly with the tip of your finger and as close to the fret wire as you can without actually being right on it. Short fingernails are important! This will create a clean tone.

RIGHT
Finger is close to the fret without actually touching it.

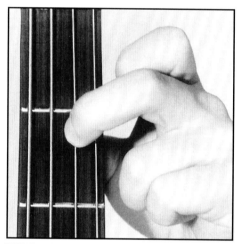

WRONG
Finger is too far from fret; sound is "buzzy" and unclear.

WRONG
Finger is on top of the fret; sound is muffled and unclear.

Tuning Your Bass

First, make sure your strings are wound properly around the tuning pegs. They should go from the inside to the outside as illustrated to the right.

Some basses have all four tuning pegs on the same side of the headstock. If this is the case, make sure all four strings are wound the same way, from the inside out.

Turning a tuning peg clockwise makes the pitch lower. Turning a tuning peg counter-clockwise makes the pitch higher. Be sure not to tune the strings too high because they could break.

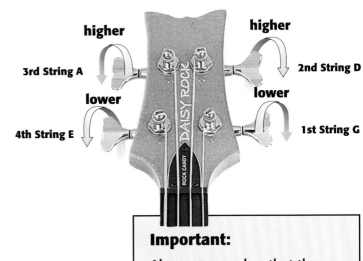

Using the CD or DVD

When tuning while listening to the CD or watching the DVD, listen to the directions and match each of your strings to the corresponding pitches.

Important:

Always remember that the thinnest, highest-sounding string, the one closest to the floor, is the first string. The thickest, lowest-sounding string, the one closest to the ceiling, is the fourth string. When bass players say "the highest string," they are referring to the highest-sounding string.

Tuning to a Piano or Keyboard

From lowest to highest, the bass is tuned to E, A, D, G, corresponding to the keys shown on the following diagram. The notes on the bass will sound an octave lower than the notes on the piano.

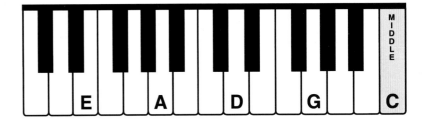

Tuning the Bass to Itself

When your fourth string is in tune, you can tune the rest of the strings using the bass alone. First, tune the fourth string to E on the piano. Then, follow the instructions below to get the bass in tune.

Press 5th fret of 4th string to get pitch of 3rd string (A).
Press 5th fret of 3rd string to get pitch of 2nd string (D).
Press 5th fret of 2nd string to get pitch of 1st string (G).

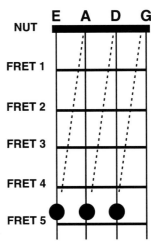

Pitch Pipes and Electronic Tuners

If you don't have a piano available, consider buying an electronic tuner or pitch pipe. There are many types available, and a salesperson at your local music store can help you decide which is best for you.

The Basics of Reading Music

Musical sounds are indicated by symbols called notes.
Their time value is determined by their color (white or black)
and by stems or flags attached to the note.

The Staff

The notes are named after the first seven letters of the alphabet (A–G), which are repeated to embrace the entire range of musical sound. The name and pitch of a note are determined by the note's position on five horizontal lines and four spaces between called the *staff*.

5th LINE

4th LINE — 4th SPACE

3rd LINE — 3rd SPACE

2nd LINE — 2nd SPACE

1st LINE — 1st SPACE

The Bass Clef

During the evolution of music notation, the staff had from 2 to 20 lines, and symbols were invented to locate a certain line and the pitch of the note on that line. These symbols were called *clefs*.

Music for the bass is written in the *bass clef*. The symbol for the bass clef is derived from the Old German way of writing the letter F. Sometimes the bass clef is called the *F clef*, because the two dots surround the 4th line of the staff to show it is the note F.

Notes on the lines: G B D F A   Notes in the spaces: A C E G

You may want to use this simple trick to remember the notes.
On the lines: **G**reat **B**ig **D**ogs **F**ight **A**nimals.   On the spaces: **A**ll **C**ars **E**at **G**as.

Measures (Bars)

Music is also divided into equal parts called *measures* or *bars*. One measure is divided from another by a *bar line*:

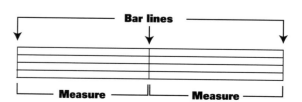

Bar lines

Measure   Measure

Counting Time

Four Kinds of Notes

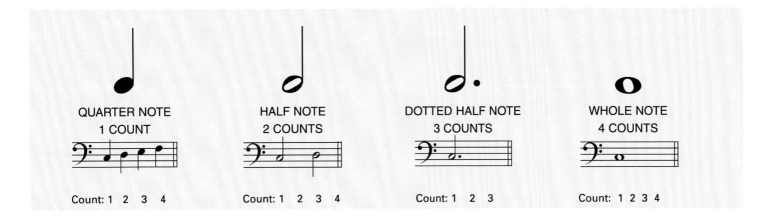

Time Signatures

Each piece of music has numbers at the beginning called a *time signature*. These numbers tell us how to count time.

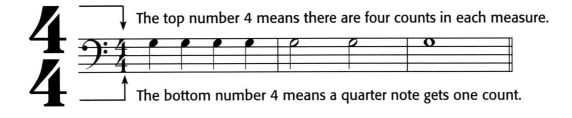

The top number 4 means there are four counts in each measure.

The bottom number 4 means a quarter note gets one count.

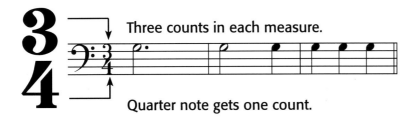

Three counts in each measure.

Quarter note gets one count.

Notes on the First String G

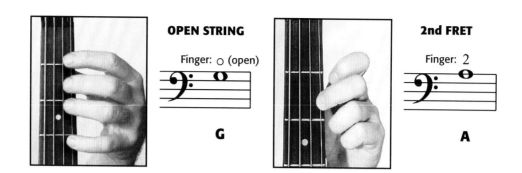

OPEN STRING
Finger: ○ (open)
G

2nd FRET
Finger: 2
A

Playing Quarter Notes *Track 2*

A double bar line indicates the end of a piece.

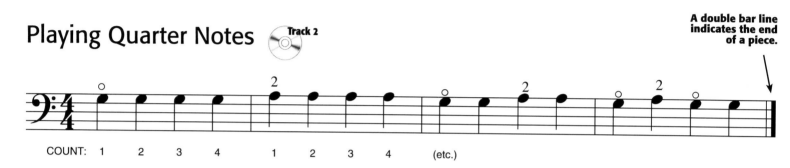

COUNT: 1 2 3 4 1 2 3 4 (etc.)

Playing Half Notes *Track 3*

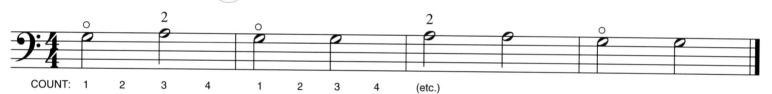

COUNT: 1 2 3 4 1 2 3 4 (etc.)

Playing Dotted Half Notes *Track 4*

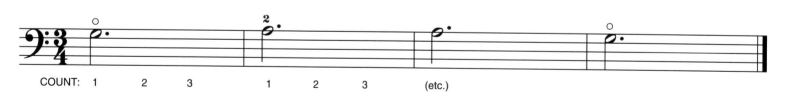

COUNT: 1 2 3 1 2 3 (etc.)

Playing Whole Notes *Track 5*

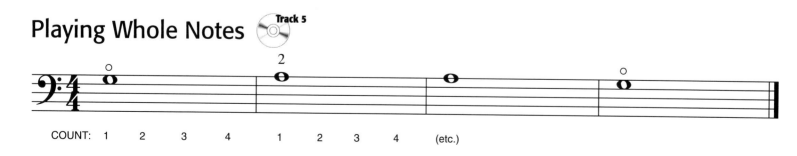

COUNT: 1 2 3 4 1 2 3 4 (etc.)

Four Rhythms in 4/4

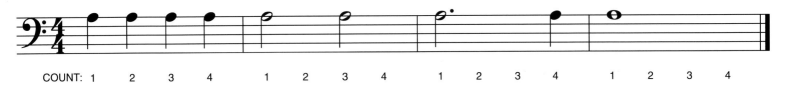

COUNT: 1 2 3 4   1 2 3 4   1 2 3 4   1 2 3 4

Four Rhythms in 3/4

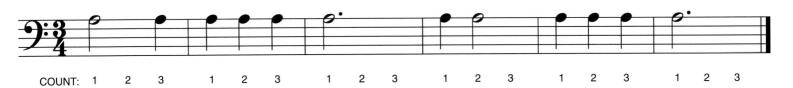

COUNT: 1 2 3   1 2 3   1 2 3   1 2 3   1 2 3   1 2 3

Mixin' It Up in Four Track 7

Continue to next line without stopping.

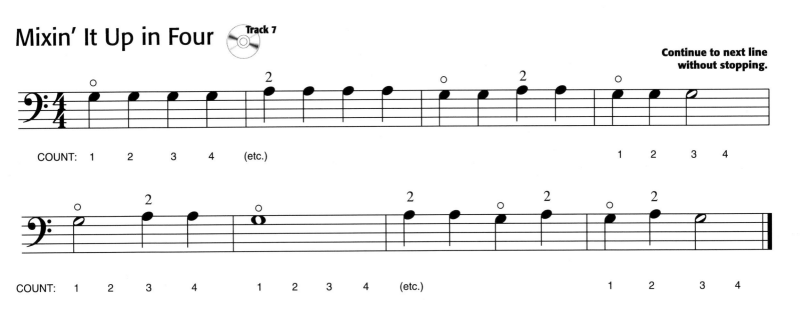

COUNT: 1 2 3 4 (etc.)   1 2 3 4

COUNT: 1 2 3 4   1 2 3 4 (etc.)   1 2 3 4

Mixin' It Up in Three Track 8

Continue to next line without stopping.

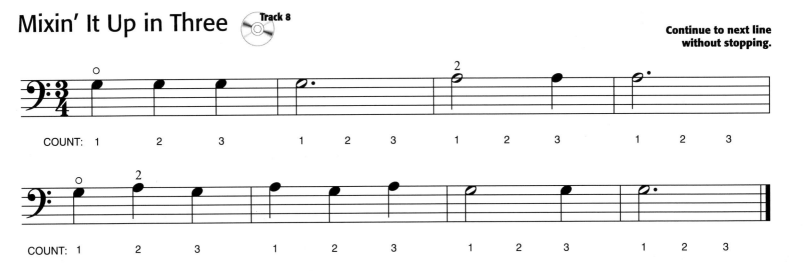

COUNT: 1   2   3   1   2   3   1   2   3   1   2   3

COUNT: 1   2   3   1   2   3   1   2   3   1   2   3

Notes on the Second String D

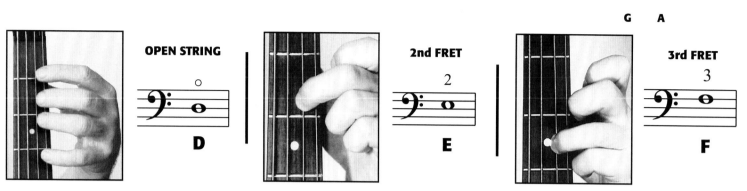

G   A

OPEN STRING — **D**   **2nd FRET** — **2** — **E**   **3rd FRET** — **3** — **F**

If you have trouble playing with the third finger alone, try adding the fourth finger until you build up strength in your third.

Playing D, E and F   Track 9

Once Again   Track 10

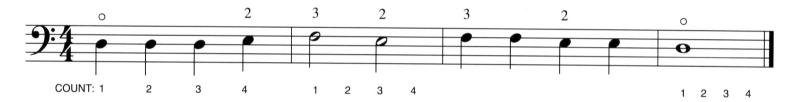

COUNT: 1 2 3 4 1 2 3 4 1 2 3 4

Extra Credit in Three   Track 11

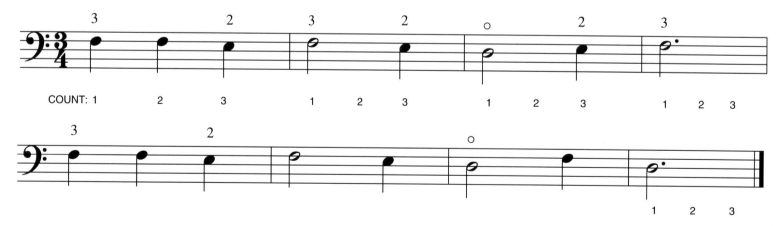

COUNT: 1 2 3 1 2 3 1 2 3 1 2 3

1 2 3

Skipping Down & Up   Track 12

COUNT: 1 2 3 4 1 2 3 4 1 2 3 4

Combining Notes On the G & D Strings

Two-String Warm-up

Here is a great daily warm-up exercise that uses the notes you have learned so far.

D Minor Blues

Here is a great bass line to use when playing a D minor blues. Chord symbols that are placed above each staff may be used for a duet. Have a friend or teacher play the chords on the guitar or keyboard while you play the bass line, or play along with the audio track on the CD or DVD. Many of the tunes in the rest of this book include chords for duets.

Notes on the Third String A

D E F G A

OPEN STRING
A

 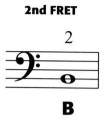
2nd FRET
B

3rd FRET
C

Up-Stems & Down-Stems

Until now, all notes have been written with the stems pointing down. To make music look neater, down-stems *and* up-stems are used:

Notes above or on the middle line have stems pointing down.

Notes below the middle line have stems pointing up.

A Few New Notes Track 15

Lookin' Up  Track 16

The A Natural Minor Scale

A *scale* is a set of eight notes in alphabetical order arranged according to a specific pattern. Scales that follow the same pattern have a characteristic sound that is distinctly different than that of other types of scales.

The *natural minor scale* in A is also known as the *Aeolian mode*. This scale includes every note you've learned so far. Play it many times as part of a daily warm-up. Keep the beat steady and get a clean sound.

Rockin' à la Mode — Track 18

A Minor Line — Track 19

Sharps

A sharp sign ♯ placed before a note means to play that note one fret higher than usual. If the note is usually played on the open string, finger the sharp note on the 1st fret with the 1st finger.

If the note is usually fingered, play the sharp note one fret higher.

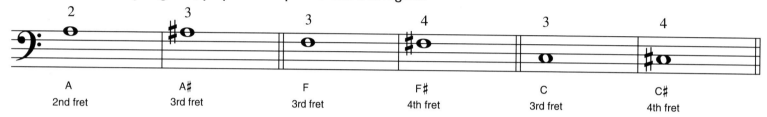

Since the note E♯ is the same as F, it is not used much. The same goes for B♯, which is the same as C.

Sharp Example No. 1

A sharp stays in effect for a whole measure.

Sharp Example No. 2

The bar line restores a sharp note to its usual position.

Naturals

A natural sign ♮ cancels a previous sharp sign in the same measure.

Notes on the Fourth Fret

You can play notes on the 4th fret with your 4th finger, or, if you do not have enough finger strength at this time, you can shift your 3rd finger up to the 4th fret.

1st STRING, 4th FRET

3 or 4

B

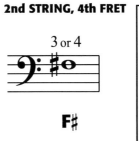

2nd STRING, 4th FRET

3 or 4

F♯

3rd STRING, 4th FRET

3 or 4

C♯

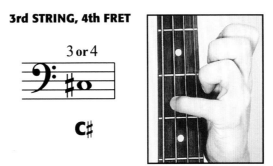

Practice these exercises that include notes on the 4th fret.

Fourth Finger Frenzy Track 22

F♯   Still F♯

Little Finger Challenge Track 23

Still G♯   Still F♯   Still C♯

Notes on the Fourth String E

NOTES YOU'VE LEARNED SO FAR

OPEN STRING

Ledger Line **E**

1st FRET **F**

2nd FRET **F♯**

The short line that extends the staff downward for E is called a *ledger line*. On a standard bass, only the low E requires a ledger line below the staff.

3rd FRET **G**

4th FRET **G♯**

E-String Strut Track 24

The E string is the largest string on the bass, which makes it the most difficult to play. Be sure to press very hard with the left hand, close to the fret (without being right on it).

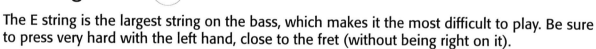

Note-Finding Review

The following exercise uses every note you've learned so far.
Practice it until you can play without missing a beat.

Swing Bass Line

Slithering Up

Octaves

You've learned the notes E, F, F♯, G, G♯, and A on the G and D strings.
You've also learned the same notes on the A and E strings, but they sound lower.
Notes that have the same letter name but sound lower or higher are in a different *octave*.
An octave is a note eight notes from another note. Think of an octopus (eight arms)
or an octet (a group of eight musicians). Octaves are an important part of bass lines
in every style of music.

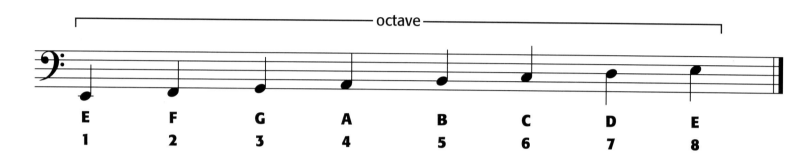

All the Octaves You Know So Far

Octave Jumps Track 28

Octabass 12

Track 29

CHORDS: A

D A

E A

Octave Boogie Lick

Track 30

MetalOctavus

Track 31

CHORDS: E5 B5

E5 B5 A5 G5 E5

Flats

A flat sign ♭ placed before a note means to play that note one fret lower than usual. For example, if the note is usually fingered at the 2nd fret, the flat note is played at the 1st fret; if the note is usually played at the 3rd fret, play the flat note at the 2nd fret.

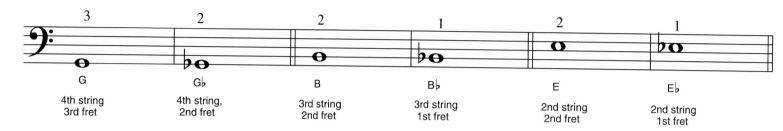

Since the note F♭ is the same as E, it's not used much. The same goes for C♭, which is the same as B

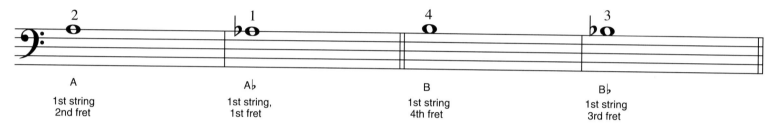

To flat an open-string note, play the next-lower string at the 4th fret.

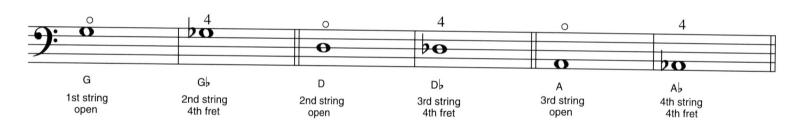

Jammin' with Sharps, Naturals & Flats 🔘 Track 32

The rules for flats are the same as for sharps: A bar line restores a flatted note to its usual position. A natural sign ♮ cancels a previous flat within the measure (and sometimes appears in the next measure as a reminder).

Practice the following exercises until you can play them without missing a beat.

Flats and Naturals

Flats, Sharps and Naturals Track 33.2

Bluesy Lick Track 34

The Key of F Major

The F Major Scale

A *major scale* is a series of eight notes in a specific arrangement of *half steps* (next fret) and *whole steps* (skip a fret). The pattern is always **W W H W W W H** (W= whole step, H= half step). The F major scale begins on F and contains a B♭.

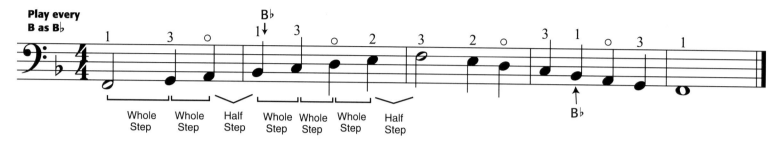

Key Signatures

Flats or sharps placed at the beginning of every staff line are known as a *key signature*. A key signature of one flat (B♭) means to play every B as a B♭, unless preceded by a natural sign. It also tells you the music is in the *key of F major*. A *key* is kind of a musical "home base" from which the music departs and eventually returns. Notice that pieces in the key of F almost always end on the note F.

The following exercise extends the F major scale to the high B♭.

The Extended F Major Scale

Rockin' in F

A repeat sign at the end of a piece means to go back to the beginning and play the entire piece again.

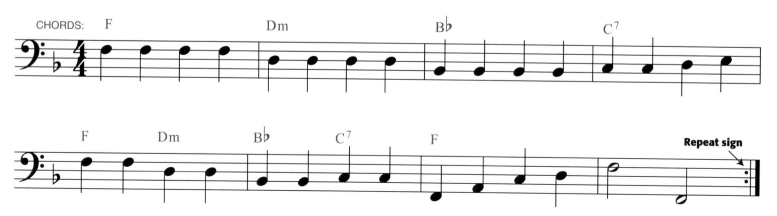

Funky Bass  Track 38

Waltz in F Track 39

Rock Ballad in F Track 40

The Key of B♭ Major

A key signature of two flats (B♭ and E♭) tells you the piece is in the *key of B♭ major*.
Unless preceded by a natural sign, all B's are played as B♭'s and all E's are played as E♭'s.

First practice the scale, then play the exercise.

The B♭ Major Scale Track 41

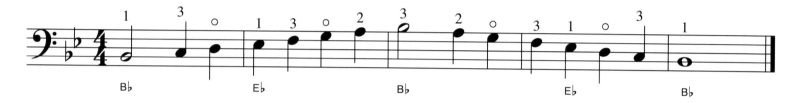

Jazz Blues in B♭ Track 42

Flats, sharps and naturals that appear in a piece but do not belong to that key (such as E♮ and A♭ in this piece) are called *accidentals*.

Bass Line

The Chromatic Scale

The chromatic scale is completely made up of half steps. When the chromatic scale is ascending, it is written with sharps; when it is descending, it is written with flats.

Ascending Chromatic Scale

Descending Chromatic Scale

Chromatic Rock

Bumble Bass

Track 48

CHORDS: Fm

Eighth Notes

Eighth notes are black notes with a flag added to the stem ♪ or ♪.
Two or more eighth notes are written with a beam connecting the stems: ♫
There are two eighth notes per beat, and eight eighth notes per measure
in 4/4 time, which are counted **1 & 2 & 3 & 4 &.**

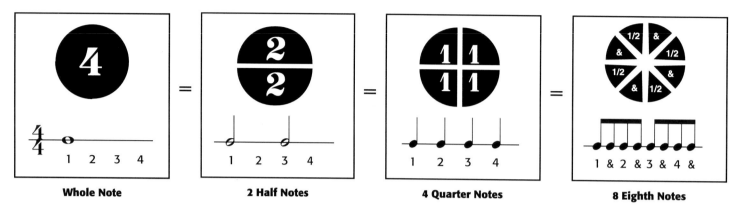

Whole Note	2 Half Notes	4 Quarter Notes	8 Eighth Notes

When playing eighth notes with your right hand, alternate between your index finger *i* and middle finger *m*.

Eighth Notes on an Open String   Track 49.1

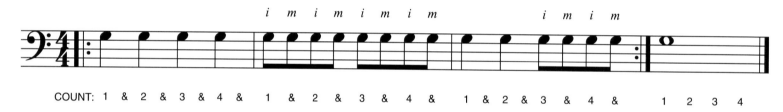

Eighth Notes on Three Open Strings   Track 49.2

Eighth Notes with Fingered Notes   Track 49.3

Quick Time

When you are fingerpicking and moving quickly from a higher string to a lower string,
try using the same finger (or *m*) to play both strings.

Early Rock with Eighths

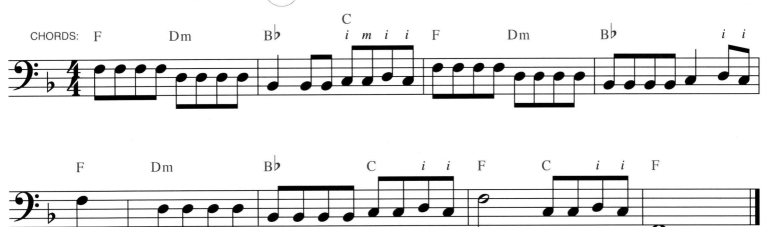

Eightude

RESTS

In music, a *rest* is a measured silence. It is important to get a clean sound when playing rests.

If the note before a rest is open, stop the vibration of the string with the fingers of the left hand.

If the note is fingered, release the pressure on the string, but keep the finger touching it.

Three Basic Rests

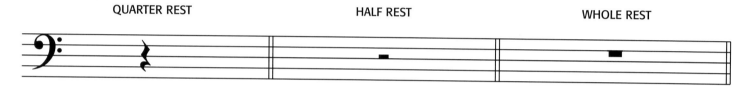

QUARTER REST	HALF REST	WHOLE REST

One beat of silence.

Two beats of silence.

A whole measure of silence (four beats in 4/4 time, three beats in 3/4 time).

An easy way to remember the difference between the half rest and whole rest is to think of the whole rest as being longer, or "heavier," and so it hangs below the line. The half rest is shorter, or "lighter," and so it sits on top of the line.

Rest Exercise No. 1   Track 53.1

COUNT: 1 2 3 4   1 2 3 4   1 2 3 4   1 2 3 4   1 2 3 4

Rest Exercise No. 2   Track 53.2

COUNT: 1 2 3 4   1 2 3 4   1 2 3 4   1 2 3 4

No Time to Rest
Track 54

Quiet Time
Track 55

Warm-ups in the Keys of F & B♭

The following exercises in the keys of F and B♭ combine eighth notes with other rhythms and make use of most of the notes you've learned so far. Serious students will want to add this page to their daily warm-ups.

Warm-up in F   Track 56.1

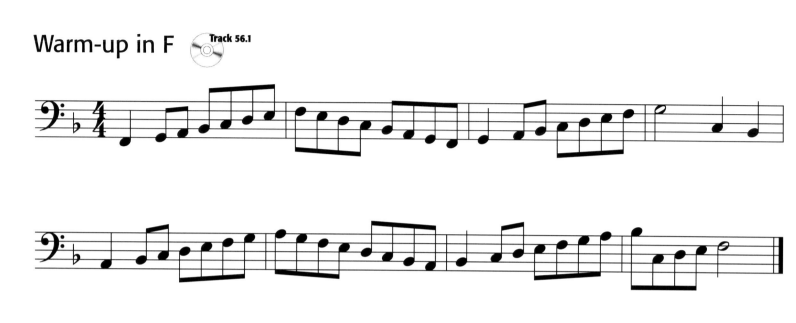

Warm-up in B♭ No. 1   Track 56.2

Warm-up in B♭ No. 2   Track 56.3

Licks in the Keys of F & B♭

A *lick* is a short phrase, usually one or two measures long, that musicians use
to fill in dead spots in the music and to add interest to their playing.

F Lick No. 1  Track 57.1

F Lick No. 2 Track 57.2

B♭ Lick No. 1 Track 57.3

B♭ Lick No. 2 Track 57.4

Second Position

All the notes you have played so far have been in *first position*, which means your left hand fingers have been placed on the first four frets. The G major scale below is in *second position*. This means that the left hand is shifted up the fingerboard so that the 1st finger plays the notes on the 2nd fret, the 2nd finger plays the notes on the third fret, the 3rd finger plays the notes on the 4th fret, and the 4th finger plays the notes on the 5th fret.

The Key of G Major

The key signature of one sharp (F♯) tells you a piece is in the *key of G major*. All F's are played as F♯'s unless preceded by a natural sign.

The version of the G major scale below is in second position.

The G Major Scale

Good King Wenceslas Track 59

Blues in G Track 60

Reading TAB

As you learn more notes in different positions, you will realize that most notes can be played in more than one place on the bass. To make it easier to recognize where to play the notes, the rest of this method will use *TAB* (short for *tablature*) in addition to standard music notation. Since most folios of popular music use TAB, it is important to know how to read TAB in addition to standard music notation. Always read the standard notation first, and then use the TAB as your guide to playing the music in the correct position.

Below each traditional music staff you'll find a four-line TAB staff. Each line represents a string of the bass, with the highest, thinnest string at the top and the lowest, thickest string at the bottom.

T	1st string (G)
	2nd string (D)
A	3rd string (A)
B	4th string (E)

Numbers placed on the TAB lines tell you which fret to play. A zero means to play the string open (not fingered).

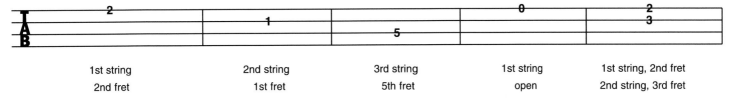

1st string	2nd string	3rd string	1st string	1st string, 2nd fret
2nd fret	1st fret	5th fret	open	2nd string, 3rd fret

By glancing at the TAB, you can immediately tell where to play a note. Although you can't tell exactly what the rhythm is from the TAB, the horizontal spacing of the numbers gives you a strong hint about how long or short the notes are to be played.

The Third Position

When playing in *third position*, shift the left hand so the 1st finger plays notes on the 3rd fret, the 2nd finger plays notes on the 4th fret, and the 3rd finger plays notes on the 5th fret.

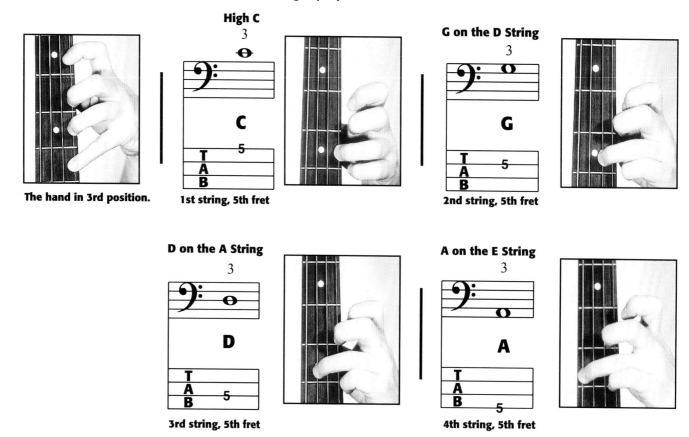

The hand in 3rd position.

High C
1st string, 5th fret

G on the D String
2nd string, 5th fret

D on the A String
3rd string, 5th fret

A on the E String
4th string, 5th fret

Notice that you now have alternate ways of playing the notes G, D, and A. Compare the following:

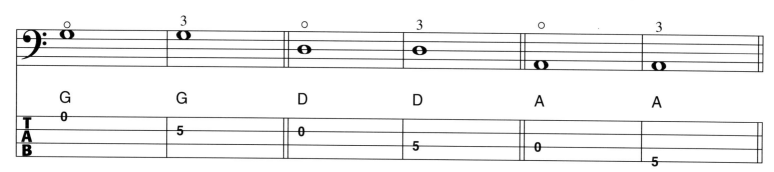

It is impossible to give a hard and fast rule about whether to use the open or fingered form of a note. Many players avoid using open strings altogether, but the best policy is to try a passage both ways and choose the form that is easier to play and produces the better sound.

For example, for the following passage, most players would find the fingering in the first measure easier to play.

41

The Key of C Major

A key signature with no sharps or flats tells you a piece is in the *key of C major*.
All notes are played natural unles s preceded by a sharp or flat.

First practice the scale, then the exercises. The fingering for some notes will change

depending on your hand position.

The C Major Scale

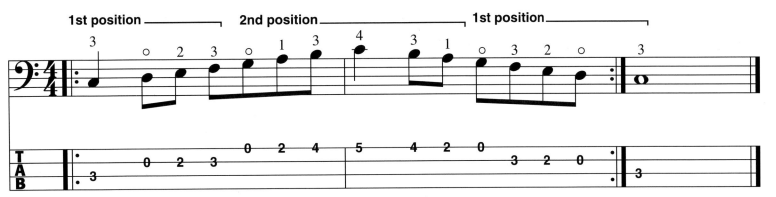

Warm-up in C

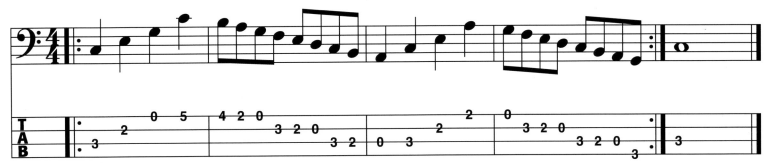

Bass Line for a Rocker

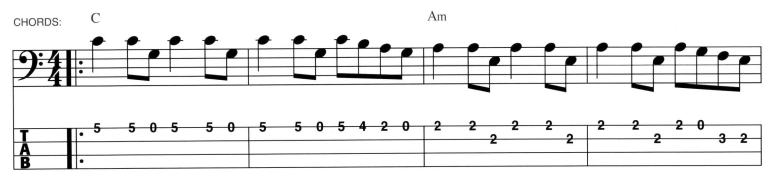

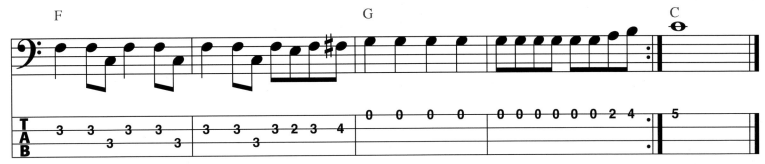

The Slide

Slide

To play a slide from a note to a higher note, pick the first note, then slide the fret finger up to sound the higher note without picking again.

Slide Up

To slide up to a note, play the string as your fret hand slides up the neck to the written pitch.

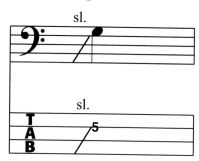

Below are some examples of slides used in country bass licks.

Slide Example No. 1   Track 64.1

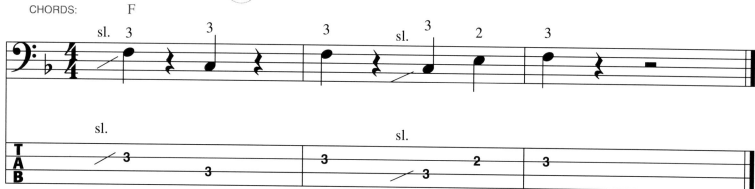

Slide Example No. 2   Track 64.2

Slide Example No. 3   Track 64.3

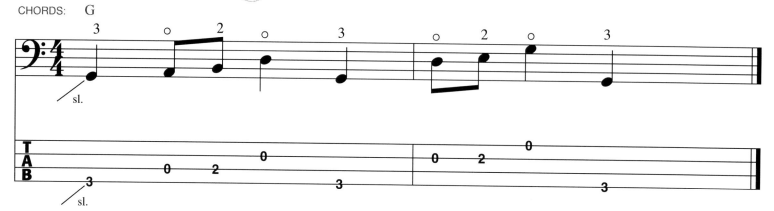

Accented Notes

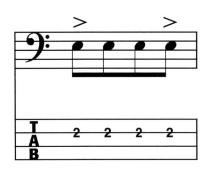

An *accent* (>) means to play a note slightly louder than usual. The picking hand plucks the string harder for an accented note than for non-accented notes.

Below are examples of accented notes used in rocka bass licks.

Accent Example No. 1 Track 65.1

Accent Example No. 2 Track 65.2

Accent Example No. 3 Track 65.3

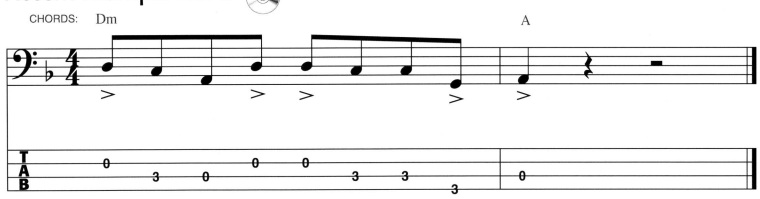

Ties & Syncopation

Ties

Ties are curved lines connecting two or more successive notes of the same pitch. When two notes are tied, the second one is not picked, but its time value is added to the value of the first note. In TAB notation, a tied note is indicated with parentheses—do not pick that note again.

Syncopation

Syncopation is a musical effect in which a note is *anticipated*, meaning it's played before its expected beat. Syncopation is critical to all types of music.

Example 1 below is not a syncopated rhythm. Each quarter note falls in the expected place, right on the beat. Examples 2–6 are various examples of syncopation.

Example 1 Track 66.1

Non-syncopated or "straight" version of the rhythm.

Example 2 Track 66.2

Beat 3 anticipated. (The third quarter note is played early, on the "&" of beat 2 rather than its expected place on beat 3.)

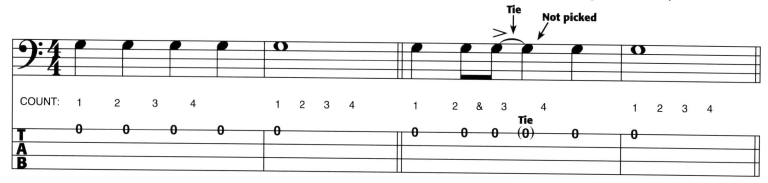

Example 3 Track 66.3

Beat 1 anticipated across the bar line.

Example 4 Track 66.4

Beat 2 anticipated.

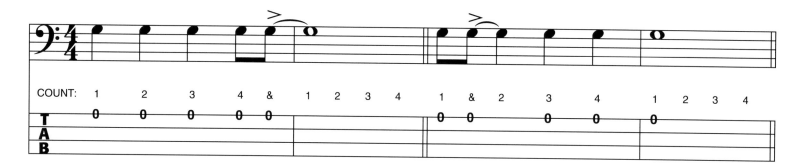

Example 5 Track 66.5

Beats 2 and 3 anticipated.

Example 6 Track 66.6

Beats 2, 3, and 4 anticipated.

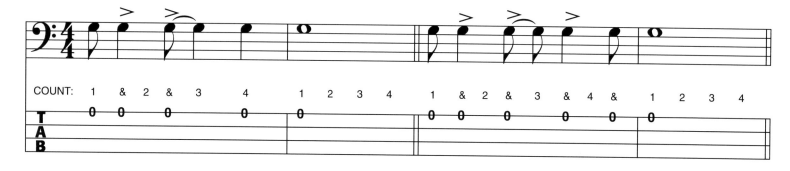

Syncopation in the Keys of C, G, F & B♭

Remember to count carefully and accent all the anticipated notes.

Syncopation Example in C Track 67.1

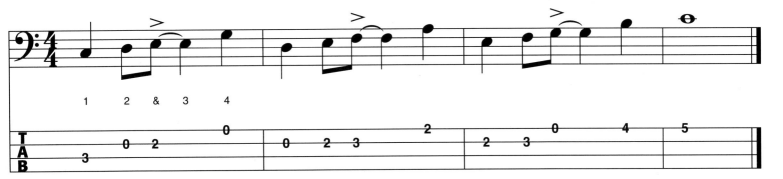

Syncopation Example in G Track 67.2

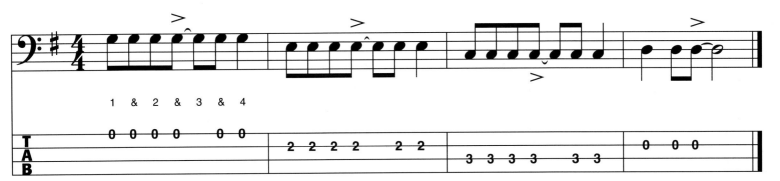

Syncopation Example in F Track 67.3

Syncopation Example in B♭

Syncopated Writing Track 68

CHORDS: C5

F5

C5

The Dotted Quarter Note

A dot to the right of a note increases its length by half. A dotted half note is equal to a half note tied to a quarter note for a total of three beats. A dotted quarter note equals a quarter note tied to an eighth note, which equals one-and-a-half beats.

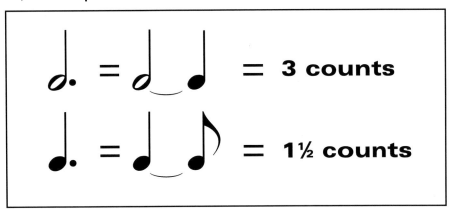

Preparatory Drill

This measure sounds the same as . . . . this measure.

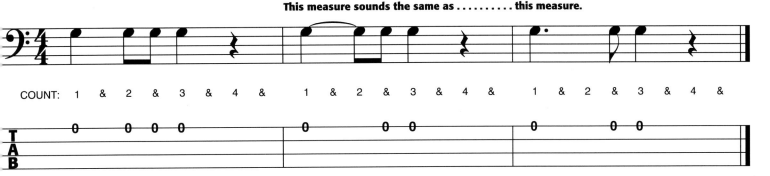

Rock Bass Line in G

Rock Bass Line in F

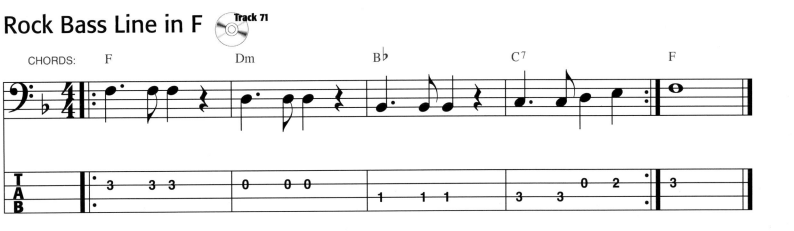

48

Combining Dotted Quarter Notes, Accents & Slides

Rock Licks with Syncopation

Rock Lick in C No. 1 — Track 73.1

Rock Lick in Bb — Track 73.2

Rock Lick in F — Track 73.3

Rock Lick in C No. 2 — Track 73.4

High C♯ (or D♭) & D

These notes further extend the upper range of notes you've learned so far. The fingering of these notes will vary depending upon the context of the music.

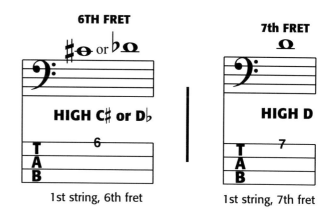

6TH FRET

HIGH C♯ or D♭

1st string, 6th fret

7th FRET

HIGH D

1st string, 7th fret

Exercise with High C♯ and D — Track 74.1

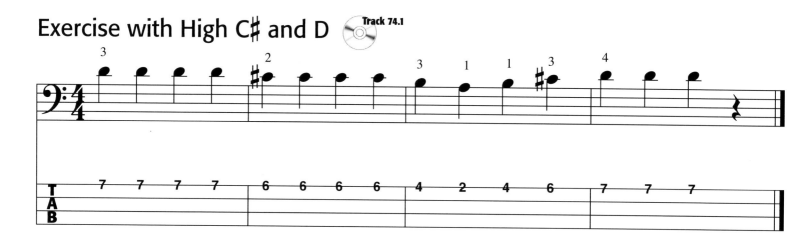

Exercise with High D♭ — Track 74.2

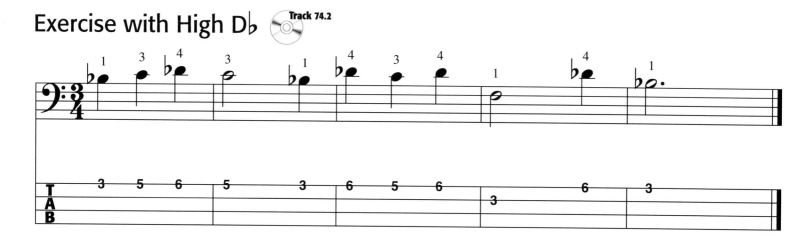

The Key of D Major

The key signature of two sharps (F♯ and C♯) tells you a piece is in the *key of D major*.
All F's are played as F♯'s and all C's are played as C♯'s, unless preceded by a natural sign.

The D Major Scale — Track 75

Joy to the World — Track 76

The D Scale in Repeated Notes — Track 77

Heavy Metal Licks in G, C & D

Heavy Metal Lick in G No. 1 Track 79.1

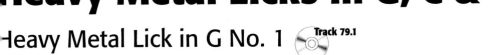

CHORDS: G

When moving up and down the neck and changing strings, it is sometimes easier to use the
4th finger to play notes usually played with the 3rd.

Heavy Metal Lick in G No. 2 Track 79.2

CHORDS: G

Heavy Metal Lick in C Track 79.3

CHORDS: C

Heavy Metal Lick in D Track 79.4

CHORDS: D

Sixteenth Notes & the Dotted 8th and 16th Note Rhythm

Sixteenth Notes

A *sixteenth note* is a black note with two flags added to the stem:

Two or more sixteenth notes are written with connecting stems:

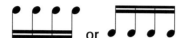

Sixteenth notes are played four to a beat, twice as fast as eighth notes and four times as fast as quarter notes.

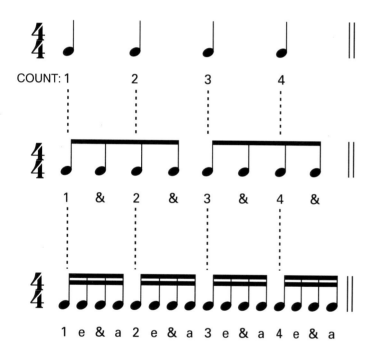

Dotted 8th and 16th Note Rhythm

The dotted 8th and 16th note rhythm is played in the time of one beat:

Count: 1 e & a 2 e & a 3 e & a 4 e & a

The dotted 8th and 16th note rhythm is used in many 1950s rock tunes and some blues. This rhythm is often called a *shuffle*. Practice the two examples below until you are comfortable with the feel.

Shuffle No. 1 Track 80.1

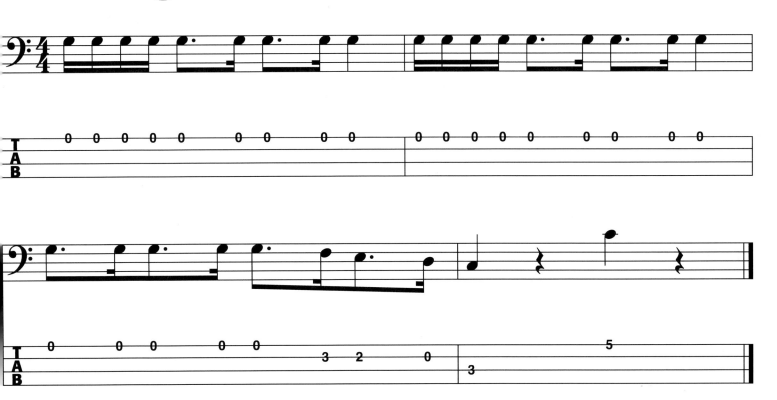

Shuffle No. 2 Track 80.2

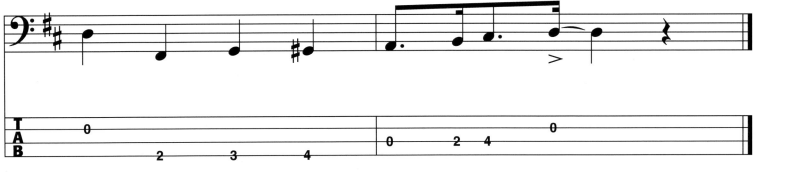

Shuffle Rhythm Bass Lines

Blues in C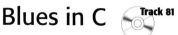

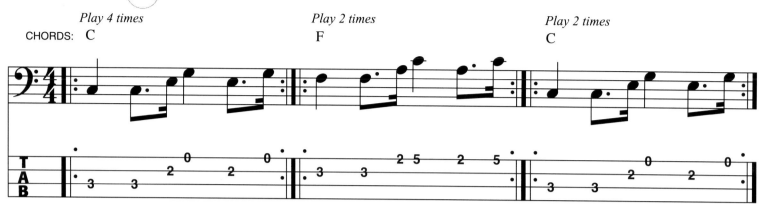

Jazzy Bass Line in D

Rockin' Line in F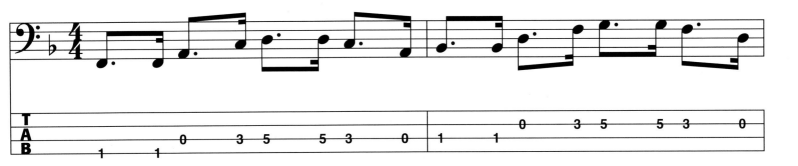
Track 83

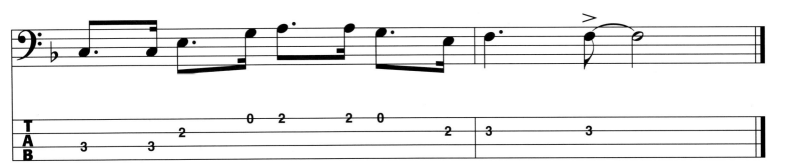

Cashin' In
Track 84

CHORDS: Am

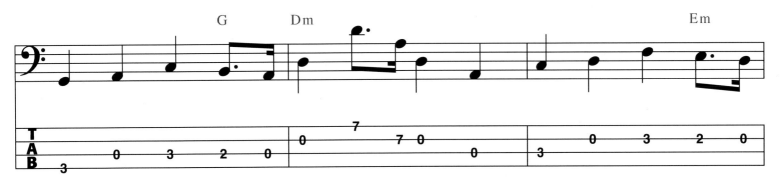

The Key of A Major

A key signature of three sharps (F♯, C♯, and G♯) tells you a piece is in the *key of A major*. All F's are played as F♯'s, all C's are played as C♯'s, and all G's are played as G♯'s, unless preceded by a natural sign. The key of A is very popular in rock and country music because it is an especially good-sounding key on the guitar.

The A Major Scale

Track 85

Incomplete Measures

Not every piece of music begins on beat 1. Music sometimes begins with an incomplete measure called a *pickup*. If the pickup is one beat, the last measure of the piece will often have three beats if it's in 4/4 time, and two beats if it's in 3/4 time.

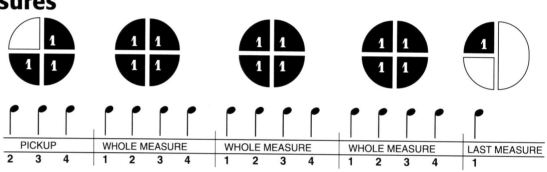

Bass Line for a Country Song

Track 86

D.C. stands for *da capo*, Italian words that literally mean "from the head." It means to repeat the entire piece from the beginning. Notice that this example begins on beat 2 of the measure. Since the last measure has only one beat, it combines with the three beats in the first measure to make one complete bar of 4/4 time.

Licks in the Key of A

The Key of E Major

A key signature of four sharps (F♯, C♯, G♯ and D♯) tells you a piece is in the *key of E major.* All F's are played as F♯'s, C's are played as C♯'s, G's are played as G♯'s, and D's are played as D♯'s, unless preceded by a natural sign.

Like the key of A, the key of E is very important in rock, blues and country music because it sounds good on the guitar.

The E Major Scale   Track 88

E Major Warm-up in 4/4   Track 89

E Major Warm-up in 3/4   Track 90

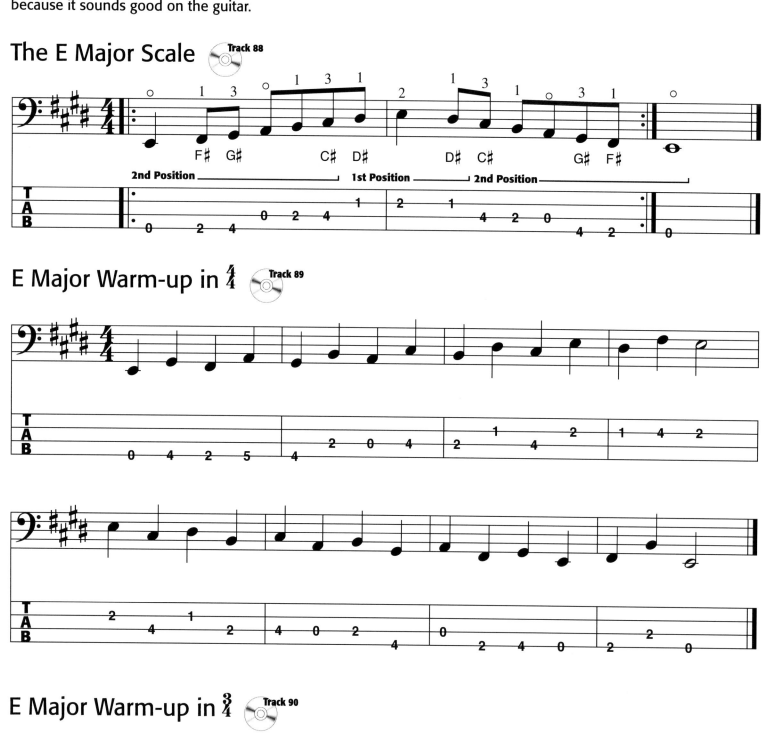

High D♯ (or E♭) & E

These notes will extend your upper register even further.

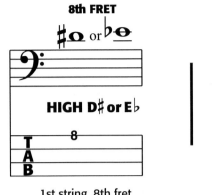 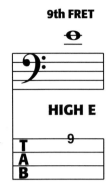

1st string, 8th fret   1st string, 9th fret

As with the notes learned on page 50, fingering depends on what precedes and what follows the note in question.

Exercise with High D♯ and E

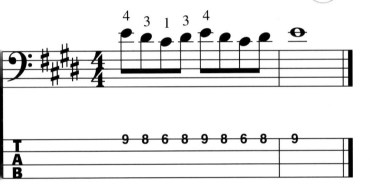

Exercise with High E♭

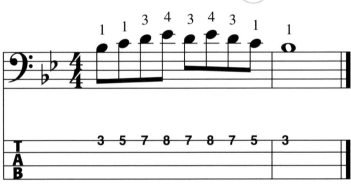

The Two-Octave E Major Scale

Your knowledge of the notes high D♯ and E allows you to play an E major scale in two octaves. Add this scale to your daily practice.

Licks in the Key of E

E Major Lick No. 1

E Major Lick No. 2

E Major Lick No. 3

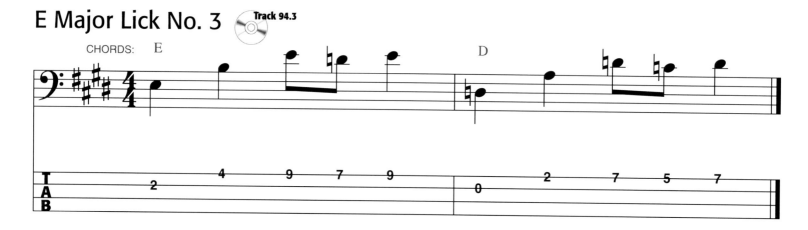

Bass Fingerboard Chart

The Bass Notes in the First Octave

The following chart shows the position of every bass note in the first octave (the first 12 frets). This includes every note used in this book as well as notes in the upper positions.

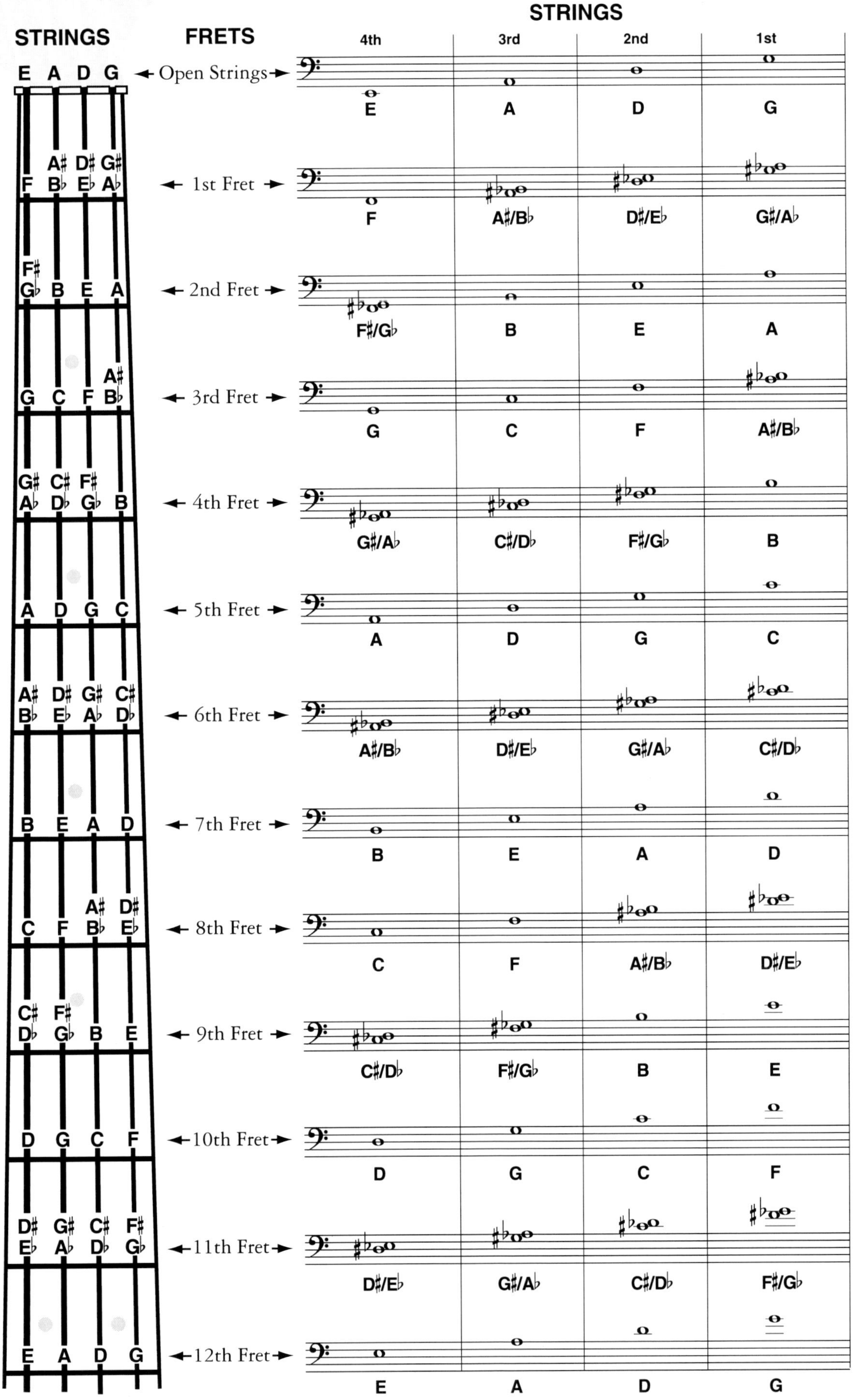

STRINGS
FRETS
STRINGS
4th 3rd 2nd 1st
E A D G
Open Strings
E A D G
1st Fret
F A♯/B♭ D♯/E♭ G♯/A♭
2nd Fret
F♯/G♭ B E A
3rd Fret
G C F A♯/B♭
4th Fret
G♯/A♭ C♯/D♭ F♯/G♭ B
5th Fret
A D G C
6th Fret
A♯/B♭ D♯/E♭ G♯/A♭ C♯/D♭
7th Fret
B E A D
8th Fret
C F A♯/B♭ D♯/E♭
9th Fret
C♯/D♭ F♯/G♭ B E
10th Fret
D G C F
11th Fret
D♯/E♭ G♯/A♭ C♯/D♭ F♯/G♭
12th Fret
E A D G

CERTIFICATE OF PROMOTION

ALFRED'S BASIC BASS METHOD 1

This certifies that

_____

has mastered
Alfred's Basic Bass Method 1
and is promoted to
Alfred's Basic Bass Method 2.

Teacher _____

Date _____